The Science of
LIVING

(The Bless Life)

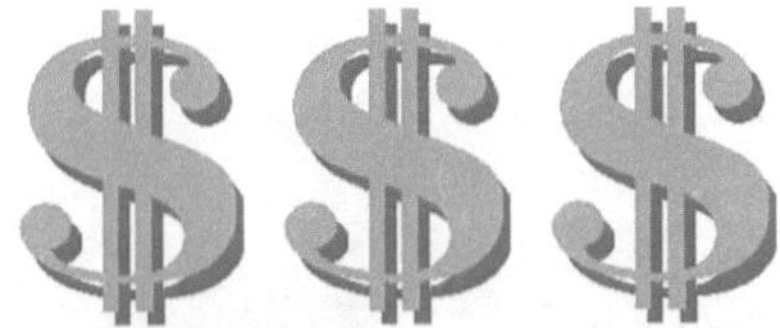

What Denominational Religions Don't Teach

Dr. L. D. Williams

ISBN 979-8-88832-220-8 (paperback)
ISBN 979-8-88832-221-5 (digital)

Christian Faith Publishing
832 Park Avenue
Meadville, PA 16335
www.christianfaithpublishing.com

Printed in the United States of America

Contents

Introduction

How This Book Came to Life

When one thinks of sciences, what comes to mind is something beyond comprehension: outer space, sci-fi, and things equated to religion. This book is designed to take an in-depth look at how science plays a part in our approach to the Word of God. The Bible says, "In the beginning God created (to cause, to happen, to bring about, and to bring into existence) the heaven and the earth," from chaos to cosmos, tracing the order of life through Yeshua/Christ. The Bible also says when a man is in Christ, he is a new creation; the old is gone and the new has come. Christ says, "I have come to give us life on earth as well as the life to come," but in the meantime, we have to live here on earth in this physical realm. In the science of living, I am becoming an esoteric specialist.

The term *esoteric* is intended for or likely to be understood by only a small number of people with specialized knowledge or interest—esoteric specialist and wisdom according to the Word of God.

> But you have the holy spirit and he lives
> within you. So, you don't need anyone to teach
> you what is true. (1 John 2:27 NLT)

For the Spirit teaches you everything you need to know, and what he teaches us is true; it is not a lie. So just as he has taught you, remain in fellowship with Christ (John 14:26 NLT).

When the Father sends the Advocate as my representation, that is the Holy Spirit; He will teach you everything and will remind you of everything. I have told you this according to James; there is a wisdom from above (within) (James 3:17).

The term *science* means knowledge that is coordinated, arranged, and systematized. So when we look at the Word of God, it's the knowledge that is coordinated, arranged, and systematized to give us a better life—a life of joy, peace, health, wealth, and superabundance.

The State of Religion

Bible Times
Pharisees
Sadducees
Herodian
Scribes
Modern-Day Religion
Catholicism
Protestant
Orthodox
Episcopalian
Judaism
Islam
Denomination
Muslim
Sunni
Shia
Baptists
Pentecostal
Methodist
African Methodist Episcopal

I'm Baptist. I'm Methodist. I'm Episcopalian. I'm Catholic. I'm Holiness. I'm COGIC. And the list goes on.

> One lord, one father, one baptism one God, and faith of all who is over all through all and in all. (Ephesians 4:5)

Now the science of living.

Chapter 1

The Science of Living

The term *science* means knowledge that is coordinated, arranged, and systematized.

The science of living is a way of thinking which gives opportunity and an open pathway to understanding oneself. It reveals the truth of who we are in God and who God is in us. The science of living teaches the presence and power of God, which is based on the Bible or the Word, not on church doctrine. The teachings and lessons of the science of living are not theology or religious dogma and tradition according to man. The Bible makes it clear in Romans 12:2 by urging us to no longer conform to the patterns of this world but to be transformed by the renewing of our minds.

We should read the Bible as those who listen to the very speech of God. (F. B. Meyer)

The way into the holistic: He has made Christ heir of all things,
And he has made you joint heir with him, and hence he has given you everything. (Charles Spurgeon)

God in the Covenant Sermon

By changing the way we think and how we use our minds, the Bible says, "If anyone is in Christ, they are a new creation; that's a new mindset, a new way of thinking, a new approach to life." The Word of God says in Proverbs 22:2,

> Rich and poor have this in common: the
> Lord is the maker of them all.

So if my old self was one of lack, poverty, and sickness, then when I come into the mind of Christ, something should change, or something is wrong, and all religion does is teach me how to lie and become a professional hypocrite. In the science of living, we move into the newness of who we are and what we are in God. I am a god with creative power. Christ was confronted with this issue. The religious leaders say, "We are not stoning you for any good work but for claiming to be God." His response:

> Is it not written in your law, "I have said you
> are gods"? If he called them gods to whom the
> word of God came, and Scripture cannot be set
> aside. (John 10:34)

In Psalm 82:6, we see our divine sonship:

> I say you are gods; you are all children of the
> most high.

And in the next verse, "we discover where we are because of religion and man-made tradition, the behavior, and the customs of the world. 'But you will die like mere mortals and fall like every other ruler.'" Now let's follow the Word.

> But to all who believed him and accepted
> Him, he gave (give) the right to become children

of God. They are reborn—not with a physical birth resulting from human passion or plan, but a birth that comes from God. (John 1:12–13 NLT)

Therefore, this new birth does not come from a man and woman or physical descent, or human effort, but by the power of God through the Spirit of God, the Holy Spirit. The new birth must first take place in you (your mind). This is not a hocus-pocus event, something magical that mysteriously brings about a change. However, this is a spiritual, mystical event when one knows or has a personal experience in which one feels as though one has been touched by a higher power or greater truth, which may occur inside or outside a religious setting. The new birth is more than being save to go to heaven; it is a reestablishing experience, opening alternatives to a supernatural dimension of life, making us worthy of living and being in the kingdom of God on earth. We are ambassadors of Christ, citizens of the kingdom of God.

The Bible says in 2 Corinthians 8:9 (NIV),

> For you know the grace of our Lord Jesus Christ, that though he was rich yet for your sake he became poor so that you through his poverty might become rich.

Theologians and worldly biblical scholars would have us believe that this passage has nothing to do with money or material wealth. They say that wealth is His self-giving, and poverty is His eternal status as Lord of heaven and earth, all the while they live wealthy, rich lives on earth and teach the people of God to be happy without. It is time for the people of God to rise and live.

> I have come that they may have life and have it superabundantly. (John 10:10b)

Chapter 2

The Science of Living Principle 1

Before you can know God, you must know who you are. We are born again as gods, not in the same sense as our Father, the Big God, but as His children, to live a life full of joy, peace, forbearance, kindness, goodness, faithfulness, gentleness, and self-control, which are the fruit of the Spirit. The Word of the Lord declares,

> My people are destroyed for lack of knowledge: "because you have rejected knowledge I also reject you as my priests because you have ignored the law of your God, I also will ignore your children." (Hosea 4:6)

This is where we were, but because of Christ, we are restored to our rightful place in God our Father. Christ is the presence of God in man; God is hidden behind Christ. Christ Jesus is the revelation of God, and man is here to reveal God to the world. Peter says in his epistle that we have been restored to a chosen people, a royal priesthood, a holy nation, God's very own possession, to show others His goodness, and He has called us out of darkness into His wonderful light (1 Peter 2:9)—food for thought.

I am to see myself as God sees me. We see the prophet Moses, the man of God, on the mountain of God. When the Lord called Moses from a blazing fire, revealing the presence of God, Moses responded, "Here I am!" (Exodus 3:4). And ten verses later, God's response to Moses, "I am that I am" (Exodus 3:14), connects "I am here" with "I am that I am," informing us not only of His name but also that "I am" is the awareness of being. When we add something to "I am," God brings it to pass. Theologians miss this concept: "I am" reproduces—you become whoever you say you are. Then we must see ourselves as being the person we desire to be, as Christ says, "I and my Father are one." Christ is the presence of God in man. "I am" are two of the most powerful words to be used with caution; our words meet us in the future.

> It is the same with my word. I send it out
> and it always Produces fruit, it will accomplish all
> I want it to, and it will prosper everywhere I send
> it. (Isaiah 55:11)

Begin to speak and see yourself as God sees us. "I am a world changer. I am a historymaker. I am a child of the Highest." And then let's remove the negative: "I am sick, I am broke, I am hurting, I am feeling bad, I am weak and lowly." "I AM" is God, and that name reproduces.

Chapter 3

The Science of Living Principle 2

God is not a man! God is often referred to as "the man upstairs," but the Bible states in Numbers 23:19,

> God is not a man, he does not lie, He is not human, so he does not change his mind. Has he spoken and failed to act? Has he ever promised and not carried it through?

This means clearly that God is not a man sitting in the sky. In the science of living, God is spirit, so those who worship Him must worship in spirit and truth. God is the spoken Word, as John 1:1 declares,

> In the beginning was the word and the word was with God.

Then God is the Word made flesh, as John 1:14 (NLT) explains:

> So the word became human and made his home among us (Within us). He was full of unfailing love and faithfulness and we have seen his glory of the Father's one and only son.

(And we are sons and daughters of God in the flesh.) The Holy Spirit, God on earth, is described in Genesis 1:2 as hovering over the surface of the water. Christ refers to the Holy Spirit as the Spirit of truth in John 16:13–15:

> When the spirit of truth comes he will guide you into all truth he will not speak on his own but will tell you what he has heard he will tell you about the future.

Chapter 4

The Science of Living Principle 3

When we realize that the power is within, then we will stop waiting for a God in the sky to do something for us. The infinite power of God is within us.

> Now to him who is able to do immeasurably more than all we ask or imagine, according to the power that is at work within us. (Ephesians 3:20 (NIV)

> To them God has chosen to make known among the gentiles the glorious, riches, of of this mystery which is christ in you the hope of glory. (Colossians 1:27)

Then Paul declares,

> Do you not know that your body is a temple of the holy spirit, who is in you whom you have receive from God? You are not your own. (1 Corinthians 6:19)

We have been taught to live through our physical senses—taste, feel, smell, hear, and see—but there is another sense we never talk about: the spiritual sense. We have the mind of Christ and the Spirit of God.

> This is what we speak, not in words taught us by human wisdom but in words taught by the spirit, explaining spiritual realities with spirit—taught words the person without the spirit does not accept things that come from the spirit of God but considers them foolishness and cannot understand them because they are discerned only through the spirit. The person with spirit makes judgement about all things, but such a person is not subject to merely human judgement for "who has known the mind of the lord to instruct him?" But we have the mind of christ. (1 Corinthians 2:13–16)

Let me reiterate this truth: Christ is the God consciousness in man. Christ is the revelation of God, and man is here to reveal God. In the book *The Mind: The Master Power*, the writer makes a distinction between the man Jesus and the title Christ, each having his own uniqueness and individuality. He says Jesus expressed completely the Christ and opened the door for us to do the same. He affirms the presence of Christ within us. To understand the work of Jesus, we must look through three lenses: Jesus is historical, theological, and psychological.

> Jesus Christ the same yesterday and today and forever. (Hebrews 13:8)

So in Christ, God must become personalized in me, through me, and as me.

Chapter 5

Science of Prayer

The term *science* means knowledge that is coordinated, arranged, and systematized. Scientific prayer is a harmonious interaction of the brain and the heart, the conscious and subconscious levels of mind, nature, and the spirit mind. By *prayer*, I do not mean the childhood model, "Now as I lay me down to sleep," kind of prayer. I mean the prayer of quietly going within yourself. Prayer is experiencing the presence of God in us and total surrender to the realization of oneness with God. Prayer is not a religious experience and is not answered by a God in the sky. Prayer is a positive mental attitude within oneself and what you say to yourself about yourself.

> If I can just touch his clothes, I will be healed. (Matthew 9:21)

When it comes to the importance of prayer, it can be easily understood when we come to know that everything and anything we possibly want in life can be received through prayer. The energy of prayer is by far greater than atomic and nuclear energy. Prayer has the ability to move heaven and earth and bring all the command that is covered under the will of God.

> It is God's will; God will answer our prayer. (Matthew 6:10)

Scripture proves that it's the will of God to answer prayer.

Ask, and God will give to you, search and you will find, knock and the door will open for you; yes, everyone who asks will receive. Everyone who searches will find, and everyone who knocks will have the door open. (Matthew 7:7–8 NCV)

If you believe you will receive whatever you ask for in prayer and faith. (Matthew 21:22)

Therefore, I tell you whatever you ask for in prayer believe that you have received and it will be yours. (Mark 11:24 NIV)

You may ask me for anything in my name, and I will do it. (John 14:14 NIV)

If you remain in me and my words remain in you, ask whatever you wish, and it will be done. (John 15:7 NIV)

Chapter 6

The Art of Prayer Must Be Mastered

Prayer is a real art that must be learned before we can receive anything and everything. We must become skilled in faith and cease all doubting; only then will prayer become a simple transaction between God the Father and His children. Prayer is simply asking and receiving from our Father, God in the highest. There is an artful and scientific way to tap into the realm of the Divine infinite power within us, allowing us to receive what we really want in life.

> Now to him who is able to do immeasurably more than we ask on imagine according to his power that is at work within us. (Ephesians 3:20)

Seeking your blessing in prayer is the art of going into the silence of cosmic power within us. Our mind and heart must be in perfect alignment to get an answer to our prayer. Art is the technique or process and the science behind the specific response of your creative mind to your mental image of thought. The technique is found in Matthew 7:7,

> Ask and God will give you. Search, and you will find. Knock and the door will open for you.

Here, it is said you will receive whatever you ask for; this statement implies the definiteness of mental and spiritual law, which indicates a direct response from the divine intelligence of our (spiritual) subconscious mind to our (natural) conscious mind. It's the thought that changes the moment, and you will change your tomorrow. Asking is receiving, according to Christ. The first letter of these three words—*ask, search, knock*—spells "A-S-K," which informs us that it's a divine fact all we have to do is *ask*. Asking presupposes a God who not only hears but answers prayers. With a proper relationship with our Father God, it becomes our legal, our redemptive, our creative right to ask and receive anything and whatever our Father has promised us, His children. And if we are His children, then we are heirs of God and coheirs with Christ, and if indeed we share in His sufferings, that we may also share in His glory.

> I consider that our present suffering is not worth comparing with the glory that will be revealed in us. (Romans 8:17–18)

Chapter 7

Science of Believing

Whatever you believe up to this point, set it aside for now. The Bible says in Romans 12:2,

> Do not conform to this world, but be transformed by the renewing of your mind. Then you will be able to test and approve what God's will is his good, pleasing and perfect will.

Now we must begin to change the way we think, not as human beings but as spiritual beings. God is spirit. The foundation from which we have been instructed says we are just mere human beings saved to go to heaven instead of hell. However, the Bible says we are little gods, born of the Big God. Somewhere, and somehow, the religion of Jesus became the religion about Him, while all the time He was proclaiming that the same Father and the same power indwelling in Him is the same Father and the same power that dwells in us. The process in John says we become children born of God. Then we are told we must be born again from humanity into divinity. Then He says you will receive power when the Holy Spirit comes upon you, informing us who we are. Now it's up to us to believe. The law of the mind is the law of belief. To believe is the way the mind works. The beliefs of one's mind are the thoughts of the mind, as simple as that. Whatever you believe with all your heart becomes possible, no matter what.

In Christ, all things are possible to them that believe, and so are the conditions of their mind, body, and circumstances, and belief can be summed up as the thoughts of the mind. It is the belief of a person that makes the difference between success and failure and between health and sickness. If you don't program your mind, the world will program it for you. We must develop a mindset as "I am out of the world business and in the business of God." The Bible says, therefore,

> Come out from them and be separate says the lord. Touch no unclean thing and I will receive you and I will be father to you and you will be my sons and daughters says the lord almighty. (2 Corinthians 6:17–18 NIV)

This takes mind power, the mind of Christ when we believe that is the Lord our God in action in us. When I believe in myself, that is the Lord our God in action. In the science of believing, we must move from the God in the sky to the God in me, who is omnipresent (present everywhere), omnipotent (unlimited power), and omniscient (knowing everything). If you want something, first get the thought in your mind or see it in your mind, and it will be yours. We must program our mind to think and believe, *I am healthy, happy, loving, successful, prosperous, and wealthy.* If we don't program our mind, the world will keep us confused. We are the master of our mind. Remember, Christ is the mastermind in us. The world says it this way, "Whatever the mind can conceive and believe, it will achieve." Go to that place in your mind where you can contact God (Matthew 6:6 NIV). Our minds must be renewed to the point that God's way becomes a natural way of thinking. "Success and prosperity is a way of thinking." Command your mind to think and believe.

Part 2

In the Science of Living

In this part of the book, I wish to deal with a delicate subject in the body of Christ and the science of church living: *money* and *prosperity*. Many argue and debate in the church and modern-day religion that money and prosperity are a curse and not the will of God, while in hot pursuit of it, and willing to lie, cheat, and steal to get it by almost any means necessary. The definition of *money* is a current medium of exchange in the form of coins and banknotes. The definition of *prosperity* is the state of being prosperous, synonymous with wealth, success, riches, well-being, and living a life of luxury, milk and honey, a bed of roses. According to *Merriam-Webster*, it is the condition of being successful or thriving; the *Cambridge English Dictionary* defines it as the state of being successful and having a lot of money. Then there's the prosperity theology, a religious belief among some Protestant Christians that financial blessing and physical wealth are always the will of God, which is called the gospel of health and wealth or success or seed faith. Now the question is why many in the body of Christ and households of faith are so stagnant, poverty-stricken, broke, busted, and disgusting, all while quoting, "My father is rich in houses and land, and owns a thousand cattle on a thousand hills." Now let's see what Christ, the science of living, and what the Bible says about the subject of money, prosperity, and blessing.

Chapter 8

The Science of Prosperity

The term *science* means knowledge that is coordinated, arranged, and systematized. The science of prosperity, interchangeable with the science of getting rich, can both be argued to be Bible-based.

> The rich and the poor have this in common:
> the Lord is the maker of them all. (Proverbs 22:2)

In the New Living Translation, Christ says in John 10:10b,

> I have come that they may have life and
> have it to the full.

Some translations say *abundantly* and *superabundantly*, making all spiritual, mental, and material riches of the universe gifts of God and from God. Here, in the *science* of prosperity, by learning and mastering the law of the mind, you can extract from God's infinite storehouse from within everything we need to live gloriously, joyfully, and abundantly. The science of prosperity and getting rich are based on the law of belief. "If you can?" says Yeshua/Christ (Jesus), "everything is possible for the one who believes." Belief is to accept sincerely as true. It is man's belief that makes the difference between poverty vs. wealth, failure vs. success, and sickness vs. health. It is a divine cosmic law that thought always produces like effects. The how-to is to believe in your heart; you can proclaim and prophe-size joy, peace, harmony, health, success, and prosperity in your now. Believe and know that our thoughts are the seeds that will grow and manifest in our experiences. You are the "I am," the gardener, and what you sow, so shall you reap. The seeds of joy, peace, success, and harmony will bring a wonderful harvest. Wealth and poverty have their origins in the mind, and a clean-cut decision must be made to inherit wealth and success. Wealth is not a matter of chance, luck, or coincidence according to the book of wisdom:

> The blessing of the lord brings wealth with-
> out trouble. (Proverbs 10:22)

The truly rich are those who use the creative power of thought and continue to impress their thoughts of wealth, abundance, and prosperity. People get rich by thinking in a certain way—the right way—according to the Word of God. It is the power of God to make rich or to make poor (1 Samuel 2:7; 1 Chronicles 29:12). More than spiritually and physically, let's become more sensible and study the Word of God from the standpoint of wealth and prosperity.

Chapter 9

Scriptural Proof that Prosperity Is in God's Will

Man was created by God to become prosperous, healthy, happy, successful, wise, and blessed with good things. He created all things good and gave them all for man to use for his own good in Genesis 1:26–30. On the sixth day, God made many promises that His children would be prosperous and happy.

Do not let the book of law depart from your
mouth, meditate day and night (Joshua 1:8)

The Bible declares in Deuteronomy 8:18 that God gives us the power to get wealth to fulfill His covenant. The Bible also speaks of the blessing of wealth used in the right way for the good of man and the glory of God. Wealth is a protector (Proverbs 10:15; 18:11); it makes many friends (Proverbs 14:20), and it makes one powerful in life (Proverbs 22:7). Unbelief, not wealth, is a great sin. There are those who advance this argument that it is not wrong to have wealth, but there are many more important blessings than wealth we need to ask for. My argument is this: it's just a mere excuse. People simply do not want to crucify old traditions, theories, and unbelief, rather than praying and asking God for financial help the same way they ask for physical and spiritual help. If people will learn the truth and ask God in faith, nothing will be impossible. Finally, so that you may be careful to do everything written in it, then you will be prosperous and successful.

> The Lord sends poverty and wealth; he humbles, exalts; he raise the poor from the dust and lifts the needed from the ash heap; he seats them with princess and has them inherit a throne of honor. (1 Samuel 2:7–8)

> And observe what the Lord your God requires walk in his ways and keep his decrees and command, his law and requirement as written in the law of Moses so that you may prosper in all you do and whatever you go. (1 Kings 2:3)

> Wealth and honor come from you: you are the ruler of all things in your hands are strength and power to exalts and give strength and power to exalt and give strength to all now, our God, we give thanks and praise you glorious name. (1 Chronicles 29:12–13)

> If they obey and serve him they will spend the rest of their days in prosperity and years in contentment. (Job 36:11)

> He is like a tree planted by streams of water which yields its fruit in season and whose leaf does not within whatever he does prosper. (Psalm 1:3)

> The lord is my shepherd I shall not be in want. (Psalm 23:1)

The lion may grow weak and hungry but those who seek the lord lack no good thing. (Psalm 34:10)

For the Lord God is a Sun and shield the Lord bestows favor and honor no good things does he withhold. (Psalm 84:11)

Who satisfies your desire with good things so that your youth is renewed like an eagle's. (Psalm 103:5)

I set before today life and prosperity, death and destruction. (Deuteronomy 30:15)

But remember the Lord your God far it is he who gives you the ability to produce wealth and so confirms his conversant, which he swore to you forefather as it is today. (Deuteronomy 8:18)

New Testament Scripture concerns prosperity:

If you believe you will receive whatever you ask for in prayer and faith. (Matthew 21:22)

Ask, and it will be given to you; seek and you will find; knock, and the door will be opened. (Matthew 7:7)

Therefore, I tell you whatever you ask for in prayer believe that you have received it and it will be yours. (Mark 11:24)

If you remain in me and my words remain in you, ask whatever you wish, and it will be given to you. (John 15:7)

But seek first his kingdom and his righteousness, and all these things will be given to you as well. (Matthew 6:33)

Give and it will be given to you. A good measure, pressed down, shaken together, and running over, will be poured into your lap. For with the measure you use, it will be measured to you. (Luke 6:38)

Remember this: whoever sows sparingly will also reap sparingly, and whoever sows generously will reap generously. Each man should give what he has decided in his heart not reluctantly or under-given and God is able to make all grace abound you so that all this at all time having all that you need you will abound in every good work. (2 Corinthians 9:6–8)

And my God will meet all your needs according you his glorious riches in Christ. (Philippians 4:19)

Beloved, I pray that in all respects you may prosper and be in good health, just as your soul prospers. (3 John 1:2 NASB)

You will be enriched in every way so that you can be generous on every occasion and through us your generosity will result in thanksgiving to God. (2 Corinthians 9:11)

Dear friends, if our hearts do not condemn us, we have confidence before God and receive from him anything we ask because we keep his commands and do what pleases him. (1 John 3:21–22)

This is the confidence we have in approaching God: that if we ask anything according to his will, he hears us. And if we know that he hears us—whatever we ask—we know that we have what we asked of him. (1 John 5:14–15)

Chapter 10

The Blessing that Brings Wealth

I have heard many definitions of the term *blessing* from many great men and women of God. Some say the blessing is the empowerment for success, while others say the blessing is the empowerment to be prosperous and to rise above. In the book of 1 Chronicles, in the fourth chapter, we meet Jabez, who asked, "Oh, that You would bless me and enlarge my territory!" And the Bible says, "And God granted his request." The word blessing first appears in the book of Genesis and again in Deuteronomy 28:1–14:

> Fully obey the Lord your God.
> All these blessings will come on you and accom-
> pany you.
> Bless in the city and the country.
> The fruit of your womb will be blessed.
> Your basket and kitchen will be blessed.
> Power over your enemies.
> Everything you put your hand to.
> Establishing you as holy.
> Will be called by the name of the Lord.
> Great wealth in everything: money, children, and land.
> Make you the banker.
> Make you the leader.
> To stay focused.

The blessing of the Lord in Psalm 112:1–8:

> Blessed are those who fear the Lord.
> Children are blessed.
> Wealth and riches are in their house.
> Even in darkness, light shines through.
> Good will follow.
> Will never be shaken and will never fear bad news.
> Our security and a winner over all.

The blessing of the Lord in Psalm 128:1–3:

> Blessed are all who fear the Lord.
> You will eat the fruit of your labor and blessing,
> and prosperity will be yours.
> Your family will be blessed.

The Blessing of the Lord in Proverbs 21:21:

> Finds life, prosperity and honor.

The blessing of the Lord in Ecclesiastes 5:19–20:

> Moreover, when God gives someone wealth and possessions and the ability to enjoy them to accept their lot and be happy in their toil- this gift from God they seldom reflect on the days of their life because God keeps the occupied with gladness of heart.

The Word of God gives us a blueprint for wealth, prosperity, joy, peace, and rest. If leaders start a new program of teaching their people, along with the people believing in the promises of God and beginning to pray and seek God for financial and spiritual blessings, God Himself will demonstrate signs and wonders in meeting every need according to their faith.

Chapter 11

Faith Makes It All Possible

Faith, as we know it, has been described as a simple form of belief, often stemming from superstition or ignorance—a viewpoint held by so-called intellectual people who believe that intellectual attainment is the highest form of knowledge acquired. They label faith, as we know it, as blind faith, only fit for women, children, and ministers, but not practical for establishing your everyday business and life affairs. Many have delighted themselves in having outgrown the so-called fairy tales of the Bible, saying the faith they have is only that which can be seen or explained by intellect.

The Apostle Paul, an intellectual and learned theologian, after years of many trials and tribulations, worked at great length on the marvelous results of growing in faith, trying to summarize in a few words that faith is the substance of things hoped for, the evidence of things not seen. In other words, faith takes right hold of the substance of things desired and brings into the world of evidence the things which were not. Paul says, speaking of faith, so that what is seen was not made out of what was visible, but out of the invisible, which leads us to understand that whatever we want is in the surrounding invisible substance, and faith is the power that can bring it out into reality for us.

There is a blind faith, for sure. It has been said that blind faith is far better than no faith at all, for by holding to it, eyes will be opened after a while. However, there is also an understanding faith. Blind faith is an instinctive belief and trust in a power higher than ourselves, whereas understanding faith is based on the immutable principle that faith does not depend on physical facts nor the evidence of senses. Faith is born of intuition from the Spirit of Truth living at the center of our being. Intuition is the unlimited boundary within our being of the invisible channel connecting every individual with God. Faith is based on truth; faith, when persisted in, brings the desired results. "To him that believes, all things are possible" (Mark 9:23). The Bible informs us in the book of Hebrews 11:6 that without faith, it is impossible to please God. Because from the moment we begin to ask, we begin to question our ability to reach God's standard of faith upon which we hang our fate. God, the invisible substance out of which all visible things are formed, is all around us, waiting to come forth into visible manifestation. God, the one creative cause of all things, is Spirit and visible awareness.

Faith, even as small as a mustard seed, gives us the power to say to the mountain of life, "Move from here to there," and it would move; nothing would be impossible. Faith that is small or weak can still accomplish the humanly impossible for God to deal with. Three things to move your mountain:

1. We all have a measure of faith; it resides within.
2. Our faith comes from hearing the good news of Christ.
3. Within us, our faith can apply to our everyday life. The just shall live by faith.

Chapter 12

We Have the Power of Affirmation

Intrinsic to the human mind is the thought that somehow it attracts to itself that which it desires. The hunger we feel is the prompting of the divine within, with the infinite longing to be filled. There exists a law of demand and supply, on the other side of which are unchangeable, faithful promises. If you believe, you will receive whatever you ask for in prayer and faith. In this law, the supply is always equal to the demand; however, there must first be a demand before the supply is utilized. To attain this position of power, we must take preparatory steps, earnestly, faithfully, and trustingly. To affirm a thing is to declare positively that it is so. There is power in our words of faith to bring all the good we desire right into our everyday lives. We speak the words and affirm them with confidence, but we have nothing to do with bringing them to pass.

> What you decide on will be done, and light
> will shine on your way. (Job 22:28)

It is God, through His own inevitable laws, who establishes the reality. The repetition of any affirmation is a necessary self-training of the mind, which has lived so long in error and false beliefs that constant repetition is needed.

There are a number of sweeping affirmations of truth:

1. God is love, life, substance, and omnipresence. God, being omnipresent (all-present), is all good, which allows us not to focus on evil, for God is also omnipotent (all-powerful). What other power can match His power? Since God is omnipresent and omnipotent, put away forever the traditional teachings of an adverse power source called the devil that can disrupt God's plan and cause harm. Do not become preoccupied with the thoughts and appearances of evil; rather, in the very presence of what seems to be evil, stand firm and affirm that God is good, always omnipotent and omnipresent, and watch the darkness flee from the light.

    Submit yourself then to God resist the devil,
    and he will flee from you. (James 4:7 NIV)

    Not stomp on his head, not rebuke, but resist.

2. Affirm, "I am a child of God, manifested in flesh, with His wisdom, power, love, and spirit flowing through me and in me. I am one with God. I and my Father are one," always remembering this affirmation. No circumstances can intervene between you and the source of wisdom, power, love, and life which is hidden in Christ, which is your Christ, the hope of glory. Nothing but our own ignorance in believing and receiving can hinder our unlimited supply.

3. "I am spirit, holy, blameless, and perfect in Christ, and nothing can harm or make us afraid because the Spirit is God and cannot become afraid or sick." So we change our attitude toward God, who is always there, by affirmation, we put ourselves in harmony with divine law, which is always working for our good and never to harm or punish, not the big bad boogeyman clergy have made Him out to be.

God so love, and God is love, but some will say what about sin, God so love the world He gave His one and only Son (the Word) (the Christ) (the Holy Spirit) to become sin for those who believe, their sin past, present, and future. No matter how weak, sick, or inefficient one may be, keep your minds, eyes, and thoughts within, with assurance and affirmations that God is good and loves us.

4.   "God is at work in us to will and to do whatever He desires to carry out, and they cannot fail." Affirm the mind of God working in us, both to will and do. It will only make us desire the good; it is our faith in God that does the work in us and through us; there can be no failure. Make affirmations with an open mind for it. God is forever in movement in regard to us, so that He manifests (all good) Himself more fully through us, and faith is the link that connects the dots of our conscious need with every moving cord of His power supply. Many have decreed and claimed their birthright by accepting their oneness with God, the creator of all that is good and loving, have learned how to become still and quiet from efforts of self and external planning and call into functioning the awesome, marvelous power of affirmation that has healed the sick, restored joy in places of pain and mourning, and has literally opened the doors of prisons and allowed prisoners to go free without one ounce of human effort or assistance.

In my research, I found a story about a man who, for five years, had been exiled from his home and country, and locked up overseas. Despite all efforts by humans and lawyers, which failed repeatedly, he decided to affirm God as his defense and deliverance. Within months, without the help of human effort or his lawyer, the doors of his prison were opened wide, and he was restored to his family and country. In another case I am aware of, a young man had joined the military, and his records had been misplaced; his superiors had no idea what to do with him. His father approached me about the matter. I suggested to the father that we were going to affirm a breakthrough on Friday night, so we called a prayer affirmation meeting. We had him write out the affirmation and prayer request, and by Monday, the records were found, an assignment was given, and he was stationed within hours of his concerned father.

Affirmations are not just the forming of words, but despite all contrary evidence, when there are no visible signs of possibility, affirmations are our oneness in body and mind with God's omnipotent power. All things are possible to those who believe. Affirmations build up and give strength, power, and courage. Therefore, I tell you, whatever you ask (affirm and claim) in prayer, believe that you have received it, and it will be yours. This is what is meant by the promise made to Joshua and the children of Israel: "I will give you every place where you set your feet." Begin to affirm that the God in me is infinite wisdom, knowledge, and power. I do not get anxious or frustrated but depend fully and trust in the principle of affirmation.

We live in our minds, and it's there where we become who God had proclaimed and anointed. In our minds, we become rich or poor, great or small. We have the power of thought to create what we want in life, also remembering the power of words is one of the greatest gifts that God has given man.

> The word that I speak are spirit and they are
> life. (John 6:63)

The transforming power of the living word becomes flesh. And we must believe that the God we serve desires for us to be happy, be joyous, and have freedom. According to Isaiah 32:18, God wants us to live in luxurious homes and wants His children to live lives that are triumphant and glorious. It is my belief that organized religion keeps God's people sin-conscious, poverty-stricken, heavenly-focused, and no earthly good, being influenced by the behavior and customs of this world, waiting for a mansion in the sky and praying to a God beyond the galaxies. The Bible says, "He became poor, so that you through His poverty might become rich." Christ Himself says, "I have come that they may have life and have it to the full" (some translations say *abundantly* and *superabundantly*). Through the science of living, it's time to take back the dominion given to us. It's time to live life to the full (more abundantly).

> Do not conform to the pattern of the world but transformed by the renewing of your mind. Then you will be able to test and approve what Gods will is his good and pleasing and perfect will. (Romans 12:2)

Scriptures and Quotations of Affirmations

I can do all things through Christ who gives me strength. (Philippians 4:13 NLT)

It is God who arms with strength and keep my way secure. (2 Samuel 22:33)

Trust in the Lord with all your heart and lean not on your own understanding; in all your ways submit to him, and he will make your paths straight. (Proverbs 3:5–6)

Call to me and I will answer you and tell you great and unsearchable things you do not know. (Jeremiah 33:3 NIV)

But those who hope in the Lord will renew their strength. They will soar on wings like eagles; they will run and not grow weary, they will walk and not be faint. (Isaiah 40:31 NIV)

My spirit rejoices in God my savior. (Luke 1:47 NIV)

The righteous person may have many troubles, but the Lord delivers him from them all. (Psalm 34:19 NIV)

You make known to me the path of life: you will fill me joy in your presence with eternal pleasure at your right hand. (Psalm 16:11 NIV)

For the Lord is a sun and shield; the lord will give grace and glory: no good thing will he withhold from them that walk upright. (Psalm 84:11)

This is the message we have heard from him a declare to you: God is light in him there is no darkness at all. (1 John 1:5 NIV)

From this command is a lamp, this teaches is a light and correction an introduction is a way to life. (Proverbs 6:23 NIV)

Whoever does not love does not know God. Because God is love. (1 John 4:8 NIV)

Your word is a lamp for my feet, a light on my path. (Psalm 119:105 NIV)

God is our refuge and strength, an ever-present help in trouble. Therefore, we will not fear, though the earth gives way and the mountains fall into the heart of the sea. (Psalm 46:1–2)

The Lord is my rock, my fortress and my savior; my God is my rock, in whom I take refuge, my shield and the home of my salvation, my stronghold. I called to the Lord who is worthy of praise and I have been saved from my enemies. (Psalm 18:2–3 NIV)

Christ is the true light of the world; it is through him alone that time wisdom is imparted to the mind. (Jonathan Edwards)

One of the greatest truths of the bible is that God loves us. And because he loves us, he wants to give us the best. (Billy Graham)

God is not a man that he should lie, nor the son of man, that he should repent has he said, and will he not do? (Numbers 23:19)

For the lord your God is God of Gods and lord of lords, the great God, Mighty and awesome, who show no partiality and accepts no bribes. (Deuteronomy 10:17 NIV)

Show me your ways. Lord teach me your paths, guide me in your truth an teach me for you are God my savior, and my hope is in you all day long. (Psalm 25:4–5)

Your kingdom come, your will be done, on earth as it is in heaven. (Matthew 6:10).

Submit yourselves therefore to God. (James 4:7).

There will be no peace in any soul until it is willing to obey the voice of God. (D. L. Moody)

God's name is so important that in heaven the very mention of it evokes worship. (Bill Bright)

Desire not to live but to praise; it is name let all your thoughts word and works tend to his glory. (John Wesley)

And we know that in all things God works for the good of those who love him, who have been called according to his purpose. (Romans 8:28 NIV)

So, faith comes hearing, that is hearing the good news about Christ. (Romans 10:17 NIV)

And without faith it is impossible to please God, because anyone who come to him must believe that he exists and that he rewards those earnestly seek Him. (Hebrews 11:6)

This message we have heard from him and declare to you: God is light in him there is no darkness at all. (1 John 1:5 NIV)

From this command is a lamp; this teaches is a light, and correction and instructions are a way to life. (Proverbs 6:23 NIV)

Whoever does not love does not know God. Because God is Love. (1 John 4:8 NIV)

Every good and perfect gift is from above coming down from the Father of the heavenly lights who does not change like shifting shadows. (James 1:17 NIV)

Whoever claims to live in him must live as Jesus did. (1 John 2:6 NIV)

In the beginning was the word and the word was with God and the word was God. (John 1:1 NIV)

Love is God's character, not simply an emotion. (David G. Beamer)

There is only one way to love God: to take not a single step without Him, and to follow with a brave heart wherever He leads. (Francis Fénelon)

This is what the Lord says—Israel's King and Redeemer, the Lord Almighty: I am the first and I am the last; apart from me, there is no God. (Isaiah 44:6 NIV)

Love the Lord your God with all your heart and with all your soul and with all your mind and with all your strength. The second is this love your neighbor as yourself there is no greater than thee. (Mark 12:30–31 NIV)

All Scripture is God-breathed and is useful for teaching, rebuking, correcting, and training in righteousness, so that the servant of God may be thoroughly equipped for every good work. (2 Timothy 3:16–17 NIV)

Since you have raised to new life with Christ, set your sights on the realities of heaven, when Christ sits in place of honor at God's right hand.

Think about things of heaven not the things of earth. (Colossians 3:1–2 NIV)

Your lord is the greatness and the power and glory and the majesty and the splendor for everything in heaven and the earth is yours. Yours, lord is the kingdom you are exalted as head overall. (1 Chronicles 29:11 NIV)

May your kingdom come and what you want done here on earth as it is in heaven. (Matthew 6:10 NCV)

I have so much to do that I shall spend that first three hours in prayer. (Martin Luther)

I close my eyes in order to see. (Paul Gauguin)

He who is filled with love is filled with God himself. (Augustine of Hippo)

Do not be anxious about anything, but in everything by prayer and petition with thanksgiving present your request to God. (Philippians 4:6)

But when you pray, go into your room, close the door and pray to your father, who is unseen then your father who see what is done I secret, will reward you. (Matthew 6:6)

Rejoice always, pray without ceasing, give thanks in all circumstances; for this is the will of God in Christ Jesus for you. (1 Thessalonians 5:16–18)

Devote yourselves to prayer, being watchful and thankful. (Colossians 4:2 NIV)

But when you ask, you must believe and not doubt, because the one who doubts is like a wave of the sea, blown and tossed by the wind. (James 1:6 NIV)

In the morning, Lord, you hear my voice; in the morning I lay my requests before you and wait in expectation. (Psalm 5:3 NIV)

Dear friends, do not believe every spirit, but test the spirits to see whether they are from God, because many false prophets have gone out into the world. (1 John 4:1 NIV)

This is how you can recognize the spirit of God: every spirit that acknowledge that Jesus Christ has come in flesh is from God. (1 John 4:2 NIV)

We accept man's testimony, but God's testimony is greater because it is the testimony it is the testimony of God which has given by his son. (1 John 5:9 NIV)

This is confidence we have in approaching God: that if we ask anything according to his will, he hears us whatever we ask we know that we have what we asked of him. (1 John 5:14–15 NIV)

I keep asking the God of our Lord Jesus Christ the glorious Father may give you the spirit of wisdom and revelation so that you may know him better. I pray also that the eyes of your heart may be enlightened in order that you may know the hope to which he has called you, the riches of his glorious inheritance in the saints. (Ephesians 1:17–18 NIV)

(Most) blessed is the man who believes in trust in and relies on the lord and whose hope and confidence the Lord is. (Jeremiah 17:7 AMP)

There to the centurions. Jesus said, go, it shall be done for you as you believed, and the servant body was restored to health at that very moment. (Matthew 8:13 AMP)

While you have the light believe in the light (have faith in it, hold to it rely on it) that you may become sons of the light and be filled with light Jesus said these things and then he went away and hid himself from them (was lost to their view). (John 12:36 AMP)

For what the scripture says? Abraham believed in (trust in) God, and it is accredited to his account as rightness (right living and right standing with God). (Romans 4:3 AMP)

Thus, Abraham believed and adhere to and trusted and relied on God and it was reckoned and placed to his account and credited as rightness as conformity to God's divine will in purpose, thought, and action. (Galatians 3:6 AMP)

So, there are three witness in heaven the Father the Word and the holy spirit and these three are one. (1 John 5:7 AMP)

Abram was very rich in livestock, in silver, and in gold. (Genesis 13:2 NKJV)

And the Lord will make you the head and not the tail; you shall be above only, and not beneath, if you heed the commandments of the Lord your God, which I command you today, and are careful to observe them. (Deuteronomy 28:13 NKJV)

Then you will prosper, if you take care to fulfill the statutes and judgments with which the Lord charged Moses concerning Israel. Be strong and of good courage; do not fear nor be dismayed. (1 Chronicles 22:13 NKJV)

When you realize there is no lacking, the whole world belongs to you. (Lao Tzu)

Religion, science, and spirituality help us make sense of the world. Life without at least one of them is a lonely and confusing place. (Naval Ravikant)

The way is not in the sky; the way is in the heart. (Buddha)

As for every man to who God has given riches and wealth and given him power to eat it to recieve his heritage and rejoice in his labor. This is the gift of God. (Ecclesiastes 5:19 NKJV)

Whoever gives to the poor will lack nothing. But curse will come upon those who close their eyes to poverty. (Proverbs 28:27 NLT)

And my God will supply every need of yours according to his riches in glory in Christ Jesus. (Philippians 4:19)

For I know the plans I have for you, plans to prosper you and not to harm you, plans to give you hope and a future. (Jeremiah 29:11)

Take delight in the Lord, and he will give you the desires of your heart. (Psalm 37:4)

Commit to the Lord whatever you do. And he will establish your plans. (Proverbs 16:3)

This book of the law shall not depart from your mouth, but you shall meditate on it day and night, so that you may be careful to do all that is written in it. For then you will make your way prosperous, and then you will have good success. (Joshua 1:8)

He holds success in store for the upright, he is a shield to those whose walk is blameless. (Proverbs 2:7)

I believe in God, but not as one thing, not as an old man in the sky. I believe that what people call God is something in all of us. (John Lennon)

The greater the doubt, the greater the awakening. (Albert Einstein)

Be guided by spirit and not driven by ego. (Unknown)

You and your purpose in life are the same thing; your purpose is to be you. (George Alexiou)

Help me never to judge another until I have walked a mile in his moccasins. (Indian Prayer)

Everything that has a beginning has an ending. Make your peace with that and all will be well. (Jack Kornfield)

Within you, there is a stillness and a sanctuary to which you can retreat at any time and be yourself. (Hermann Hesse)

The soul is placed in the body like a rough diamond, and must be polished, or the luster of it will never appear. (Daniel Defoe)

If a man is to live, he must be all alive, body, soul, mind, heart, and spirit. (Thomas Merton)

And God blessed them, and God said to them, "Be fruitful and multiply and fill the earth and subdue it, and have dominion over the fish of the sea and over the birds of the heavens and over every living thing that moves on earth." (Genesis 1:28 KJV)

For God so loved the world, that he gave his one and only son, that whosoever believes in him shall not perish, but have eternal life. For God did not send his son to condemn the world but to save the world through him. (John 3:16–17 NIV)

You must find the place inside yourself where nothing is impossible. (Deepak Chopra)

The power within you is greater than the power within the world. (Rhonda Byrne)

Knock, and he'll open the door vanish and he'll make you shine like the son. Fall and he'll raise you to the heavens, become nothing and he'll turn you into everything. (Rumi)

We are not human beings having a spiritual experience. We are spiritual beings having a human experience. (Pierre Teilhard de Chardin)

The most important time in the world is the time you make for yourself. (Unknown)

There is neither past nor future. There is only the present. (Unknown)

When God is your reason to live, you will never have a reason to give up. (Unknown)

Step out of the circle of time and into the circle of love. (Rumi)

Music is the mediation between the spiritual and the sensual life. (Ludwig van Beethoven)

I have set the Lord always before me; because he is at my right hand, I shall not be moved. (Psalm 16:8 AMP)

For me to live I Christ [his life in me] and die is gain [the gain of glory of eternity]. (Philippians 1:21 AMP)

For God is not unrighteous to forget or overlook your labor and the love which you have shown for his name sake I ministering to the needs of the saints (our consecrated people), as you still do. (Hebrews 6:10 AMP)

If they obey and serve him, they shall spend their days in prosperity and their years in pleasantness and joy. (Job 36:11 AMP)

Let those who favor my righteous cause and have pleasure in my uprightness shout for joy and be glad and say continually, "Let the lord be magnified who takes pleasure in the prosperity of his servant." (Psalm 35:27 AMP)

Prosperity and welfare are in his house, and his rightness endure forever. (Psalm 112:3 AMP)

In the day of prosperity be joyful but in the day of adversity consider that God has made the one side by side with the other so that man may not find out anything that shall be after him. (Ecclesiastes 7:14 AMP)

Oh, that you had hearkened to My commandments! Then your peace and prosperity would have been like a flowing river, and your righteousness [the holiness and purity of the nation] like the [abundant] waves of the sea. (Isaiah 48:18 AMP)

If the plan doesn't work, change the plan, but never the goal. (Author unknown)

"For I know the plans I have for you," declares the Lord, "plans to prosper you and not to harm you, plans to give you hope and a future." (Jeremiah 29:11 NIV)

Do not those who plot evil go astray? But those who plan what is good find love and faithfulness. (Proverbs 14:22 NIV)

Just as a candle cannot burn without fire, men cannot live without a spiritual life. (Buddha)

Be guided by spirit and not driven by ego. (Unknown)

Prayer is friendly conversation with the one we know loves us. (St. Teresa of Avila)

The way is not in the sky; the way is in the heart. (Buddha)

The great thing to remember is that though our feelings come and go, God's love for us does not. (C. S. Lewis)

I want to be just a pure spiritual leader. (Dalai Lama)

Early in the morning they left for the desert of Tekoa, as they set out, Jehoshaphat stood and said, "Listen to me, Judah and people of Jerusalem! Have faith in the Lord your God and you will be upheld; have faith in his prophets and you will be successful." (2 Chronicles 20:20 NIV)

See, he is puffed up; his desires are not upright—but the righteous will live by his faith. (Habakkuk 2:4 NIV)

If you continue in your faith, established and firm, and do not move from the hope held out in the gospel. This is the gospel that you heard and that has been proclaimed to every creature under heaven, and of which I, Paul, have become a servant. (Colossians 1:23 NIV)

Fight the good fight of the faith. Take hold of eternal life to which you were called when you made your good confession in the presence of many witnesses. (1 Timothy 6:12 NIV)

And how from infancy you have known the holy Scriptures, which are able to make you wise for salvation through faith in Christ Jesus. (2 Timothy 3:15 NIV)

I have fought the good fight, I have finished the race, I have kept the faith. (2 Timothy 4:7 NIV)

Pray that you may be active in sharing your faith, so that you will have a full understanding of every good thing we have in Christ. (Philemon 6 NIV)

Blessed are all who fear the Lord, who walk in his ways. You will eat the fruit of your labor; blessings and prosperity will be yours. (Psalm 128:1–2 NIV)

You will pray to him, and he will hear you, and you will fulfill your vows. What you decide on will be done, and light will shine on your ways. (Job 22:27–28)

He prays to God and finds favor with him. He sees God's face and shorts for Joy he is restored by God to his righteous state. (Job 33:26 NIV)

Honor the Lord with your wealth, with the firstfruits of all your crops; then your barns will be filled to overflowing, and your vats will brim over with new wine. (Proverbs 3:9–10)

He is like a tree planted by streams of water, which yields its fruit in season and whose leaf does not prosper. (Psalm 1:3 NIV)

He will be like a tree planted by the water that seeds out it roots by the stream. It does not fear when heat comes; it leaves and always green. It has no worries in a year of drought and never fails to bear fruit. (Jeremiah 17:8 NIV)

God, after he spoke long ago to the Father in the prophets in many portions and in many ways in these last days has spoken to us in his son whom he appointed heir of all things through whom also he made the world. (Hebrews 1:1 NASV)

For God is not unjust to forget your work and the love which you have shown toward his name in having ministered and in still ministries to the saints. (Hebrews 6:10 NASB)

Devote yourselves in prayer with an alert mind and a thankful heart. (Colossians 4:2 NLT)

So be careful how you live. Don't live like fools, but like those who are wise. (Ephesians 5:15 NLT)

Again, the kingdom of heaven is like a fishing net that was thrown into the water and caught fish of every kind. (Matthew 13:47 NLT)

I am writing to you who are mature in the faith because you know Christ who existed from the beginning, I am writing to you who are young in the faith because you have won your battle with the evil. (1 John 2:13 NLT)

I have written to you who are God's children because you know the father I have written to you who are mature in the faith because you know Christ who existed from the beginning I written to you who are young in the faith, because you are strong. God's who live in your hearts and you have won your battle with the evil one. (1 John 2:14 NLT)

Therefore if any man is in Christ, he is a new creature the old thing has passed, behold new things have come. (2 Corinthians 5:17 NASB)

For our struggle is not flesh and blood, but against the rulers, against the power, against the power, against the world forces of this darkness, against the spiritual forces of wickedness in the heaven's places. (Ephesian 6:12 NASB)

I pray that the eyes of your heart may be enlighted so that you may know what the hope of his calling is what are the riches of the glory of his inheritance in the saints. (Ephesians 1:18 NASB)

For Christ did not enter a holy place made with hands, a mere copy of the true one, but into heaven itself, now to appear in the presence of God for us. (Hebrews 9:24 NASB)

For the law, since it had only shadow of the good things, can never by the same sacrifices year by year which they offer continually make perfect those who draw near. (Hebrews 10:1 NASB)

Do not love the world nor the things in the world. If anyone loves the world, the love of the Father is not in him. (1 John 2:15 NASB)

God writes the gospel not in the bible alone, but also on trees, and in the flower and clouds and stars. (Martin Luther)

I believe and therefore anything is possible. (Unknown)

Whatever your heart clings to and confides in, that is really your God. (Martin Luther)

I love the Lord, for he heard my voice; he heard my cry for mercy. (Psalm 116:1 NIV)

O Lord, I call to you; come quickly to me. Hear my voice when I call to you. (Psalm 141:1 NIV)

Keep me safe, O God, for in you I take refuge. (Psalm 16:1 NIV)

Come, let us sing for joy to the Lord; let us shout aloud to the Rock of our salvation. (Psalm 95:1 NIV)

O Lord, the God who saves me, day and night I cry out before you. May my prayer come before you; turn your ear to my cry. (Psalm 88:1 NIV)

How good and pleasant it is when brothers live together in unity! (Psalm 133:1 NIV)

About the Author

Dr. L. D. Williams was born in Orangeburg, South Carolina, and grew up in the nation's capital, Washington, DC. Dr. Williams is a graduate of Faith Bible College and Seminary. Dr. Williams received his doctorate in leadership, a master of divinity, and a bachelor of arts in biblical studies and pastoral theology. Dr. Williams served as Second Vice President of the National Association Council of Community Churches of America and elsewhere. He is the organizer and Pastor of Divine Prosperity Worship Center. Dr. Williams is a certified personal trainer through the ISSA (International Sports Sciences Association). Dr. Williams is currently studying metaphysics.